Piano / Vocal / Guitar

CHART HITS OF

MW01242297

ISBN 978-1-4234-7381-7

HAL•LEONARD®
CORPORATION
7777 W. BLUEMOUND RD. P.O. BOX 13819 MILWAUKEE, WI 53213

Visit Hal Leonard Online at
www.halleonard.com

BETTER IN TIME

Words and Music by ANDREA MARTIN
and JONATHAN ROTEM

Recorded a half step higher.

BREAKOUT

Words and Music by TED BRUNER,
TREY VITTETOE and GINA SCHOCK

DISTURBIA

Words and Music by CHRIS BROWN, BRIAN SEALS,
ANDRE MERRITT and ROBERT ALLEN

Moderate Techno-Pop

it can con-trol ___ you. It's too close for com-fort, oh. ___ / I feel like a mon-ster, oh. ___ Throw on your

brake ___ lights, ___ we're in the cit-y of won-der. Ain't gon' play ___ nice. ___ Watch out, you

just might go un-der. Bet-ter think twice, ___ your train of thought will be al-tered. So

if you must fal-ter, be wise. ___ Your mind's in dis-tur-bi-a. ___ It's like the

FALL FOR YOU

Words and Music by
JOHN VESELY

The best thing 'bout to-night's _ that we're not fight - ing. Could it be _

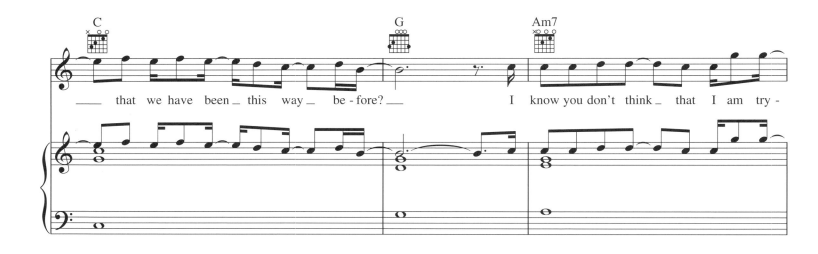

_ that we have been _ this way _ be - fore? _ I know you don't think _ that I am try-

- ing. _ I know you're wear - ing thin _ down to the core. _ But

24

GIVE ME YOUR EYES

Words and Music by JASON INGRAM
and BRANDON HEATH

*Recorded a half step lower.

HOT N COLD

Words and Music by MAX MARTIN,
LUKASZ GOTTWALD and KATY PERRY

With energy

You change your mind ___ like a girl ___ chang-es clothes.
We used to be ___ just like twins, ___ so in sync.

Yeah, you P. M. S. ___ like a bitch,
The same en-er-gy ___ now's a dead ___

___ I would know. ___ And you al-ways think,
bat-ter-y. ___ Used to laugh ___ 'bout noth-ing, ___

I'M YOURS

Words and Music by
JASON MRAZ

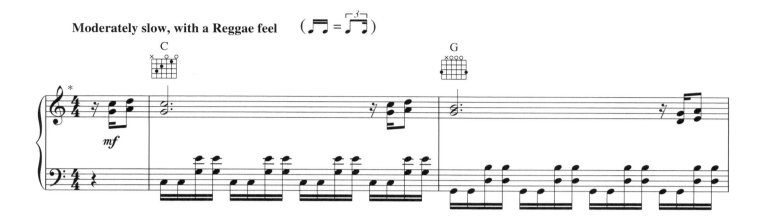

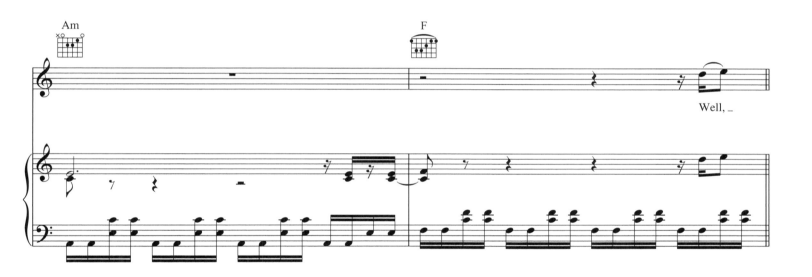

Well, _

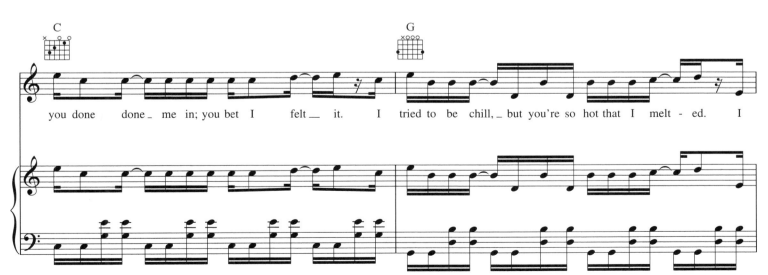

you done done _ me in; you bet I felt _ it. I tried to be chill, _ but you're so hot that I melt - ed. I

*Recorded a half step lower.

42

more. __ It can - not wait. I'm yours. _____

Well, o - pen up your mind and see __ like me. __ O - pen up your plans and, damn, __ you're free.

more. __ It can - not wait. I'm yours. _____

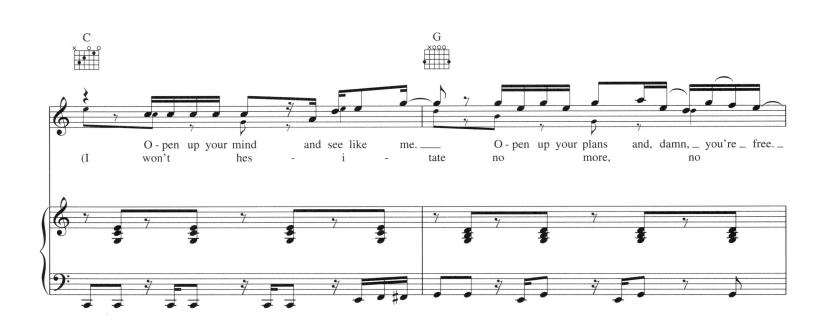

O - pen up your mind ___ and see like me. ___ O - pen up your plans ___ and, damn, __ you're __ free. __
(I won't hes - i - tate no more, no

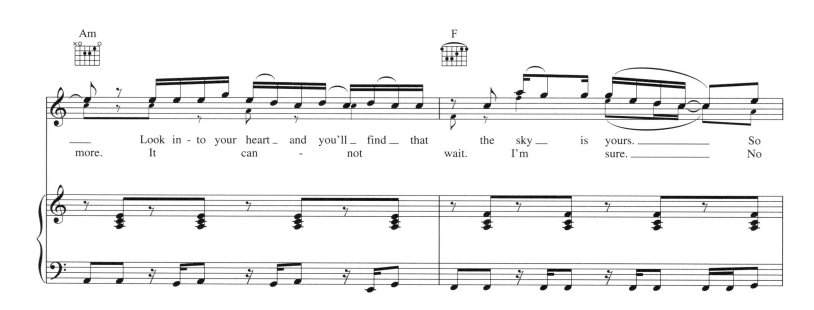

___ Look in - to your heart __ and you'll __ find __ that the sky __ is yours. _____ So
more. It can - not wait. I'm sure. _____ No

I DON'T CARE

Words and Music by PETER WENTZ,
PATRICK STUMP, JOSEPH TROHMAN,
ANDREW HURLEY and NORMAN GREENBAUM

JUST DANCE

Words and Music by STEFANI GERMANOTTA,
RedOne and ALIAUNE THIAM

KEEPS GETTIN' BETTER

Words and Music by CHRISTINA AGUILERA
and LINDA PERRY

Driving Shuffle

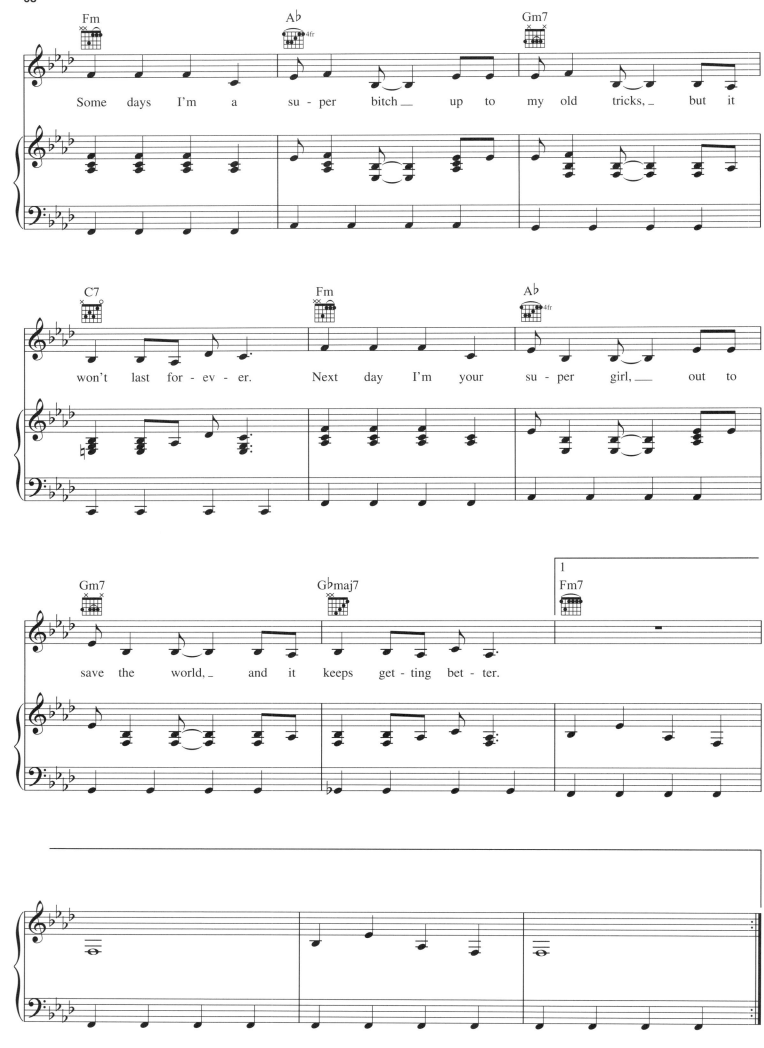

A LITTLE BIT LONGER

Words and Music by
NICHOLAS JONAS

Moderately slow

Got ___ the news ___ to-day; ___ doc-tor said ___ still ___
___ this time ___ goes by,

___ I had ___ to stay ___ a } lit-tle bit long-er and I'll ___ be fine. ___
___ no rea-son why. A

When I thought ___ it'd all ___ been done, ___ when I thought ___
Wait-ing on ___ the cure, ___ but ___ none ___

But you don't ___ know what ___ you've got ___ 'til ___ it's gone, ___

and you don't ___ know what ___ it's like ___ to feel ___ so

LOVE STORY

Words and Music by
TAYLOR SWIFT

Moderately

D(add9)

We were both young when

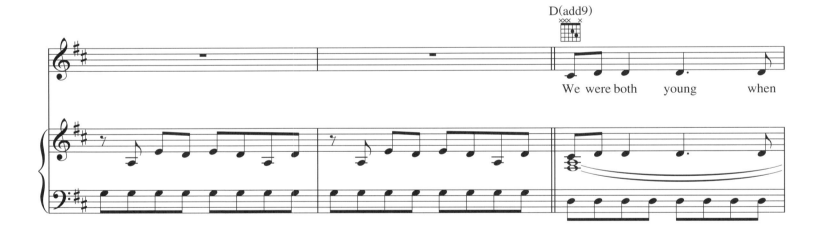

Gsus2

I first saw __ you. I close my eyes __ and the flash-back starts. __ I'm stand-in'

LOVEBUG

Words and Music by NICHOLAS JONAS,
JOSEPH JONAS and KEVIN JONAS II

REHAB

Words and Music by JUSTIN TIMBERLAKE,
TIMOTHY MOSLEY and HANNON LANE

Recorded a half step higher.

MY LIFE WOULD SUCK WITHOUT YOU

Words and Music by LUKASZ GOTTWALD,
MAX MARTIN and CLAUDE KELLY

Up-beat Pop

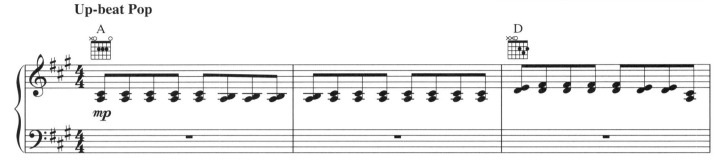

Guess this means _ you're sor - ry, you're
May - be I _ was stu - pid for

stand - ing at _ my door. _ Guess this means _ you take _
tell - ing you _ good - bye. _ May - be I _ was wrong _

THE SHOW

Words and Music by LENKA KRIPAC
and JASON REEVES

I'm just a lit-tle bit caught in the mid-dle, life ___ is a maze,

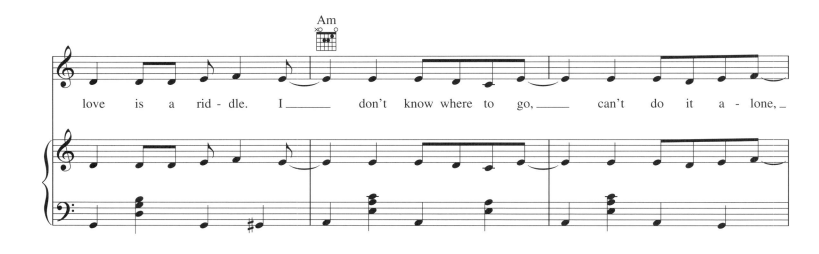

love is a rid-dle. I ___ don't know where to go, ___ can't do it a-lone, ___

___ I've tried, ___ and I don't know ___ why. _____

SINGLE LADIES
(Put a Ring on It)

Words and Music by BEYONCÉ KNOWLES,
THADDIS HARRIS, CHRISTOPHER STEWART
and TERIUS NASH

Moderate groove

All __ the sin-gle la-dies, __ all __ the sin-gle la-dies. __ All __ the

sin-gle la-dies, __ all __ the sin-gle la-dies. __ All __ the sin-gle la-dies, __ all __ the sin-gle la-dies. __ All __ the

sin-gle la-dies, __ now put your hands up.

Up in the club, we just broke up. I'm
gloss for my lips, a man on my hips, hold me

120

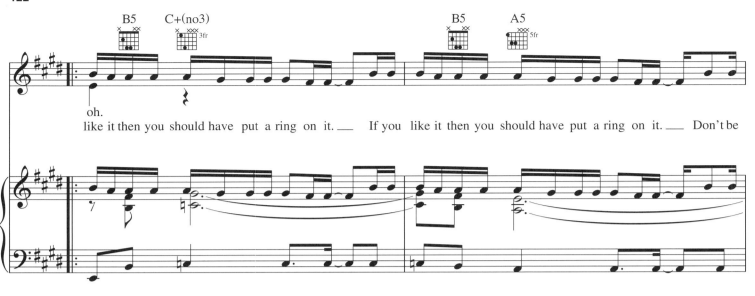

oh.

like it then you should have put a ring on it. ___ If you like it then you should have put a ring on it. ___ Don't be

mad _ once you see ___ that he want it. ___ If you like it then you should have put a ring on it. Oh, oh,
'Cause if you

like it then you should have put a ring on it. Oh, oh, oh.

VIVA LA VIDA

Words and Music by GUY BERRYMAN, JON BUCKLAND,
WILL CHAMPION and CHRIS MARTIN

124

YOU FOUND ME

Words and Music by JOSEPH KING
and ISAAC SLADE

Moody Rock

I found God _ on the cor - ner of First _ and Am - i - stad

where the West _ was all but won. _

All a - lone, _ smok - ing his _ last cig - a - rette. I said,

* Recorded a half step lower.

to the cor - ner of First __ and Am - i - stad. _____

Lost and in - se - cure, _____ you found __ me, you found __ me.

Ly - ing on __ the floor, _____ sur - round - ed, sur - round - ed.

Why did you have to wait? _____ Where were __ you, where were __ you?

WHAT ABOUT NOW

Words and Music by DAVID HODGES,
BEN MOODY and JOSH HARTZLER

D.S. al Coda